1&2 SAMUEL
SURVIVING THE TENSIONS OF LIFE

JAMES C. DANT

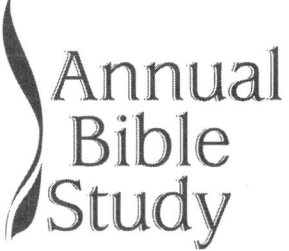

Study Guide

SMYTH&HELWYS
PUBLISHING, INCORPORATED MACON, GEORGIA

CONTENTS

Annual Bible Study

Cecil P. Staton, Jr.
President

David L. Cassady
Executive Vice President /
Publisher

Lex Horton
Vice President, Editorial

Mark K. McElroy
Senior Editor

P. Keith Gammons
Editor

Kelley F. Land
Assistant Editor

Jean Trotter
Associate Editor

Jim Burt
Art Director

Barclay Burns
Vickie Frayne
Dave Jones
Graphic Design

Cover art
David. Andrea del Verocchio. 1470.
Bronze. Museo Nazionale de Bargello.
Florence, Italy.

1-800-747-3016 (USA)
1-800-568-1248 (Canada)

SMYTH&HELWYS
PUBLISHING INCORPORATED   MACON, GEORGIA
WWW.HELWYS.COM

   Preface............................. 4

1 *Surviving Political Tension* 7

2 *Surviving Theological Tension* 20

3 *Surviving Relational Tension*............... 33

4 *Surviving Spiritual Tension*................ 46

PREFACE

First and Second Samuel are tense books. Don't let that scare you away. I imagine you probably have enough tension in your life already. Most of us traverse the turmoil of car pools, bottom lines, deadlines, and a to-do-list so long that . . . well, it's surprising you even found time to pick up this study guide. The tensions of 1 and 2 Samuel, however, were recorded in order to help us deal with the tensions in our lives.

Writing this study guide was a practice in dealing with tension. How does one address fifty-five biblical chapters, four major characters, and centuries of Israelite history in four short sessions of study? How can we revisit moments in the life of ancient Israel and find relevance for a twenty-first-century culture? It is possible. In fact, I found my journey through the Books of Samuel to be tense, but at the same time, a journey to be treasured.

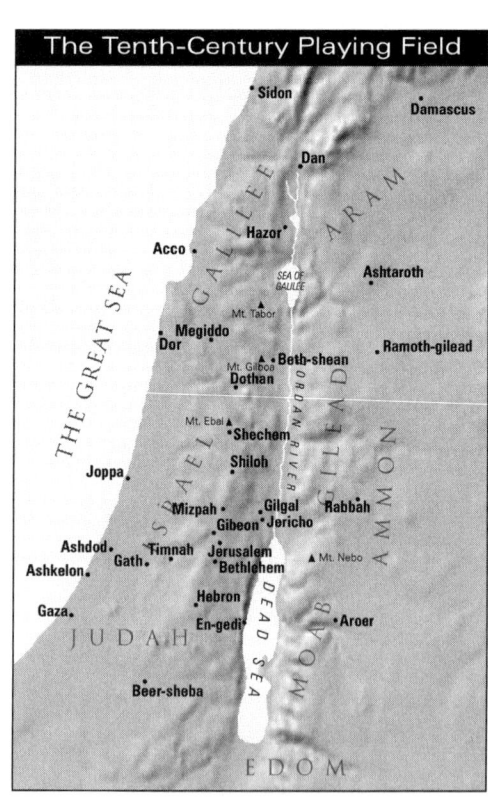

Structure eases tension. A detailed agenda can gently guide an otherwise tumultuous committee meeting. A carefully constructed itinerary can allow the most anxious of travelers to relax. While the issues in 1 and 2 Samuel are not always comfortable, the chapters in this study guide are formatted to make your journey through the various tensions as comfortable as possible.

Each chapter of this study guide has three divisions: *The Occurrence, The Memory,* and

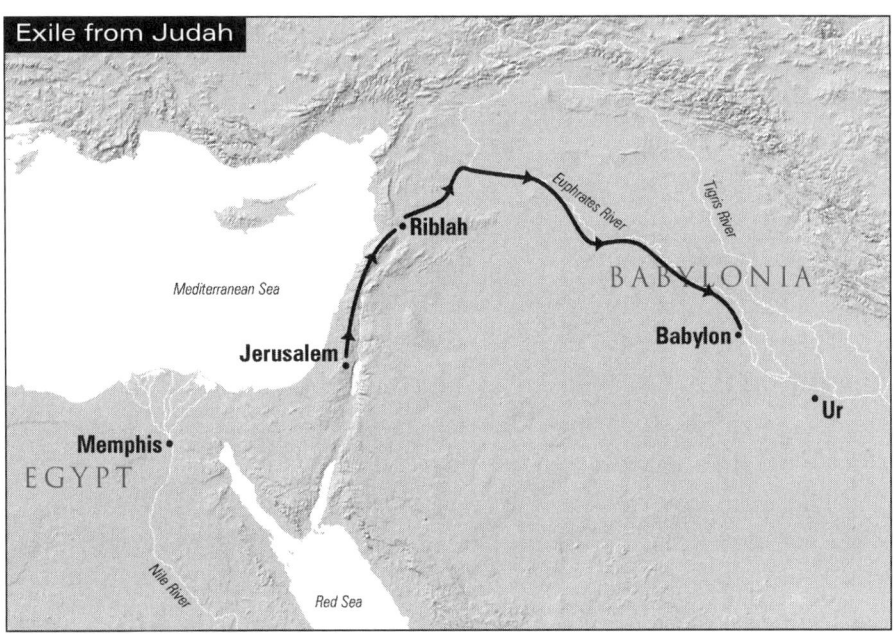

The Interpretation. These divisions have been developed to help you engage and manage the fifty-five chapters, four characters, and centuries of history contained in the text of 1 and 2 Samuel. (You can do it. Really, you can.) The three divisions support the underlying assumption that the stories in 1 and 2 Samuel occurred in the eleventh and tenth centuries BC, but were purposefully retold and recorded in their present form around the sixth century BC. They occurred during the prosperous reigns of Kings Saul and David. They were recorded during the Babylonian exile—a time when the Israelites were a displaced and enslaved nation.

The Occurrence helps the reader understand the period in which the stories of 1 and 2 Samuel actually happened. A selected focal text introduces us to one of the four main characters of 1 and 2 Samuel, as well as the particular tension with which they struggled. Each of the four chapters focuses on a different character. A detailed analysis of the focal text is presented. Particular attention is given to how the text relates to the particular tension discussed.

The Memory guides the reader to focus attention on the era in which these stories were remembered. While they certainly have historic significance in their occurring context, the greater significance of these stories may be found in the context of when they were recalled, retold, and recorded. This chapter leads the reader to view the focal text, as well as other stories from the featured character's life, through the eyes of the enslaved Israelite. Several questions dominate this portion of our journey: Why were these stories recalled during the Babylonian exile? What do these stories teach us about God and about Israel? How did these stories bring peace and hope to a suffering people?

Finally, *The Interpretation* helps relate the truths and tensions in these ancient texts to our contemporary lives. Each division ends with questions and/or activities designed to reinforce the information you have addressed. This final division ends, however, with activities that are more personal and applicable in nature. After all, if these stories brought hope and peace to the ancient lives of an enslaved people, then maybe—just maybe—they can also bring hope and peace to the tense and tumultuous times of *our* lives.

Sharing these stories and engaging these questions with you is not a task I could accomplish alone. My family—Sonya, Lauryn, Meggie, and Holly—has been supportive and understanding of my self-imposed exile during the completion of this project. The members of my second family—Gerald Carper, Cass DuCharme, Carol Brown, Ruth DuCharme, and Billie Chapman—have been invaluable guides in the respective areas of instrumental music, choral music, educational theory, children's educational resources, and the operation of various office machines. Many others, including the wonderful congregation at Highland Hills Baptist Church in Macon, Georgia, have patiently prayed, encouraged, listened, and dialogued. I am thankful to each of them for being a part of my life story.

Chapter One

SURVIVING POLITICAL TENSION

SAMUEL: DEVOTED BUT DEVASTATED

Focal Text: 1 Samuel 8:1-22   Broader Text: 1 Samuel 1–15

If you skipped the Preface to this study guide, go back and read it now. Really . . . I'll wait for you. While the final paragraph of the Preface contains the usual thank-yous that many readers intentionally ignore, the earlier paragraphs include historic and structural information that will enable you to navigate this study guide more comfortably.

Did you finish the Preface? Now, if you haven't read all fifty-five chapters of 1 and 2 Samuel, take a moment to read them. Okay, this time I'm kidding. If you have the time, however, I would encourage you to read the complete text of 1 and 2 Samuel. There is no substitute for a thorough, even casual, reading of the entire text. My first journey through both books was on an airplane between Atlanta, Georgia, and Newark, New Jersey. I made it through most of 1 Samuel and into 2 Samuel. I finished 2 Samuel later that evening.

I was amazed at everything I had missed during my earlier years of "hit-and-miss" reading in these prophetically historic books. Sunday school and seminary had left gaps in my acquaintance with these books. (Actually, the extent to which I applied myself in Sunday school and seminary produced the gaps.) While I was familiar with the call of Samuel, the anointing of David, the killing of Goliath, the adultery with Bathsheba, and the death of Absalom, there was a host of other stories—rich stories—that I had somehow missed.

I was also unaware of the inherent tension that exists in the Books of Samuel. In the award-winning film *Forrest Gump*, the more active moments of the movie are separated by scenes of Forrest sitting on a park bench telling his story. After each segment of tension, the viewer is allowed to relax a while with Mr. Gump and reflect upon the significance of what they have seen and heard. There is no park bench in 1 and 2 Samuel. These books move from altar to home to cave to wilderness to palace to battlefield and back again. Causes and consequences lead to more causes and consequences. The reader is always on the move—tense.

The characters you will meet also create this inherent tension. Not only are Samuel, Saul, David, and the God of Israel unique within themselves, but their interactions with one another create vivid and often vicious tension. This element of interaction is not as prevalent in other biblical literature. The Book of Judges, which precedes 1 and 2 Samuel, allows one judge to complete a term of service before another judge is appointed. In 1 and 2 Kings, which follows the Books of Samuel, kings rule in succession after the death of the king that preceded them. But in the Books of Samuel, the four primary characters often coexist—struggling for power, purpose, and attention.

A survey of both books will also make you aware of the tension present in their structure. Over and over again, it appears that someone has collected these stories and arranged them in such a way that the tensions of Israel's existence are highlighted. For instance, in 1 Samuel 7, Samuel the judge has been successful in using his office to keep the enemy Philistines under control. In 1 Samuel 8, immediately following the successes of chapter 7, the Israelites call for a new system of government to deal with national enemies; they want a king instead of a judge. While there were certainly other events that occurred between these two moments in Israelite history, these instances are placed side by side in obvious tension.

The editor(s) of these stories is most often referred to as the Deuteronomic Historian. In the years that led to and through the Babylonian exile, the Historian compiled Israel's history in the books of Deuteronomy, Joshua, Judges, Samuel, and Kings. The stories that were remembered and recorded convey the political, theological, relational, and spiritual tensions that were a part of Israel's past. These same four tensions were present during the Babylonian exile, the period in which these stories were remembered. Perhaps there is healing in the recollection of how God has helped us in the past. We shall see.

THE OCCURRENCE

First Samuel 8 is pivotally situated between two distinct periods in the history of Israel: the period of the Judges and the era of the united monarchy. Eugene Peterson, author, pastor, and professor, has called it "one of the most change-charged times in Israel's history."[1] It was a time of tense transition from the theocratic government of Israel's past to the monarchical government of Israel's future.

Theocracy refers to a governmental system in which the leadership is considered divinely inspired. It was this loose and faithful form of government that Israel had embraced since its exodus from Egypt. God served as their king and simply, yet mysteriously, operated through chosen individuals like Moses, Joshua, Gideon, Deborah, Samson, and eventually Samuel. These individuals all served at the whim and will of God. They were not chosen or empowered by the people. Often, they were not even appreciated by the people. But they were God's chosen instruments, participants in the theocracy and divinely inspired.

Times change, however. By 1 Samuel 8, the children of Israel are no longer the wandering slave population depicted in Exodus and Deuteronomy. They are more than just a loose confederacy of tribes that settled the promised land under Joshua. They have moved beyond the nomadic and village existence prevalent in the early days of their lives in Canaan. As often happens when people settle, the population increased, other cultural groups were amalgamated into society, wealth was accumulated, cities and institutions were established, and all of this led to a need for defense.[2]

The sporadic emergence of judges at the divine whim and will of God did not provide the kind of consistency the Israelite population felt they needed. This old system did not seem to meet their new societal and institutional identity. So the people asked for a king.

1 Samuel 8:1-5. These first five vv. of 1 Samuel 8 record Israel's request for a king as well as the reasons that precipitated the request. The historic narrator informs us of Samuel's age and his sons' lack of credibility in vv. 1-3. The Israelite elders reiterate both pieces of information in their address to Samuel in vv. 4-5.

Historically, Samuel is the last of the divinely appointed judges. Since Israel's conquest of Canaan, God had appointed judges to make necessary governmental decisions and muster necessary troops for defense. This system of governance was a purposeful alternative to the oppressive government they had experienced in Egypt.[3] Sabbath, feasts, and freedom took the place of pharaohs, bricks, and whips. The Israelites had decided to orient their lives under the complete rule and leadership of God. But it seems this new generation of Israelites had forgotten the potential dangers that dwell in human power. They wanted a king.

The elders added another reason for their monarchical request, however. In v. 5, they not only refer to Samuel's age and sons as reasons for wanting a king, but they also reveal a desire to be like the other nations. This desire was contrary to the heritage and identity they received at Mt. Sinai following their exodus from Egypt.[4] The Laws of Moses were established to make them a unique people. They were to live under God's rule, by God's care, and within God's protection. But to a generation decades removed from the powerful exodus experience, and faced with Samuel's sons as apparent heirs to judgeship, the request for a king made practical sense

In fact, one wonders if Samuel had even begun to doubt the extent of God's activity in the life of Israel. Verse 1 indicates that Samuel had appointed his sons judges over Israel. This is inconsistent with the prior divine selection of judges. Samuel's appointment of his own sons sounds strangely similar to the story concerning Eli's appointment of his sons in 1 Samuel 2. It appears that both judges extended power to unqualified children. This nepotistic conveyance of power was much more consistent with monarchical practice. It is easy to see why the people felt comfortable asking for a king since Samuel and his predecessor had already cracked the door.

1 Samuel 8:6-18. Samuel is displeased by the elders' request for a king. He apparently takes their request as a personal assault upon his performance and position as judge of Israel. Samuel had been devoted to God and devoted to the people. Now, it appeared the people were rejecting him. It was true that he was aging. It was also true that his sons were unfit successors. But God had always provided through the theocratic system in the past and Samuel felt the people should trust the system today. Samuel had been a devoted judge, but in 8:6, he is devastated.

God, however, interpreted Israel's desire for a king as divine rejection. God assures Samuel, in v. 7, that the people had not rejected Samuel, but rather rejected the role of king personified in God. God had served as Israel's king, but they wanted a visible, tangible, and manageable king like the other nations.

In v. 9, God instructs Samuel to warn the people of the harsh realities of royal power. Walter Brueggemann, noted Old Testament scholar, has called 1 Samuel 8:10-18, "the harshest, most extensive criticism of monarchy in the Old Testament" and "one of the most important pieces in the Old Testament on the abuse of public power."[5] It describes in candid detail the physical and spiritual consequences Israel will endure at the hands of a human king.

> **Palace Provisions**
> According to 1 Kgs 4:22-23, the provisions needed to feed Solomon's court with bread and meat alone for *a single day* amounted to 300 bushels of choice flour, 600 bushels of meal, 10 grain-fed oxen, 20 pasture-fed cattle, and 100 sheep, not to mention unnumbered deer, gazelles, roebucks, and grain-fed fowl. One can only imagine the number of farmhands, butchers, cooks, and attendants required to maintain the flocks and fields and to prepare and serve the meals.

Physically, taxation and confiscation will define their existence. Verses 11-17 vividly state that the king will take Israel's sons for military and agricultural purposes, daughters for his private domestic service, property and produce for the benefit of the monarchy, and cattle and flocks to add to add to his wealth and the provision of the palace. And the final result of all this taking? "[Y]ou shall be his slaves" (v. 17). The monarchy will exist by confiscation and its goal will be the king's well-being rather than the welfare of the people.

Samuel's warning did not end here, however. There was a spiritual price to pay as well. Verse 18 indicates that God's role will change in relationship to Israel. The climactic warning states, "in that day you will cry out because of your king . . . but the LORD will not answer you in that day." Israel's historic pattern of communication with God would be broken. While in Egyptian slavery, Israel cried out to God and Moses was sent. At the edge of the Red Sea, Israel cried out to God and a great wind parted the waters. In the face of the Philistines, Israel cried out to God and Samson arose as a great warrior judge. But the spiritual consequence of Israel's desire for a king was the reality that God would no longer participate in the dialogue of rescue. The people must live with and rely upon the power they have chosen.

1 Samuel 8:19-22. Samuel did what every good prophet is supposed to do. He brought the word of the Lord to the people. He sermonically warned them of the physical and spiritual consequences of their chosen direction. Israel did what most congregations do; they ignored the words of the prophet. In vv. 19-20, the people resound what the elders had earlier explained—they wanted a king like the other nations. The people, in fact, were more explicit in their description of the imagined benefits of this king. He will "govern us, go out before us, and fight our battles." Their argument was a direct contradiction of God's warning to them. For God had said their sons would man the king's chariots, they would run before the king's chariots, and the king would appoint others to fight his wars (vv. 11-12). Often our dreams of "the way things will be" rarely coincide with reality. Kings rarely fight wars for people; it's usually the other way around.

The people's refusal to change the direction of their desires prompts another conversation between Samuel and God. Samuel conveyed to God the predictable message—they will not listen. God conveyed to Samuel an unpredictable message—"Listen to their voice and set a king over them" (v. 22).

God's instruction to Samuel was quite possibly the climax of Samuel's sense of devastation. The judge, who had been so resistant to the transition from theocracy to monarchy, had now been asked to administer the process. It was difficult enough that the people had not listened. It was difficult enough that the people had forgotten Samuel's successful past. But now, God had acquiesced. Rather than punishing the people or propping up his prophet, God gives in. And so, there is another system on the horizon.

God has chosen to manage the life of Israel in a different manner. God has elected to lend credence to a structure that Samuel opposed. Was God being weak? Was God being graceful? Was God still in control? Samuel was devoted but devastated. And he still had a lot to learn about God.

A Brief History of Israel

To understand better when the stories of 1 and 2 Samuel actually occurred and when they were recalled and recorded, review the following brief history of Israel:

PERIOD	DATE	RELATED TEXTS	SYNOPSIS
Primeval	c. pre-2000 BC	Gen 1–11	Israel does not exist.
Patriarchal	c. 2000–1700 BC	Gen 12–50	Israel is a family.
The Exodus	1280–1250 BC	Exod–Deut	Israel is a population of freed slaves.
Conquest of Canaan	1250–1200 BC	Josh	Israel enters the land of promise.
The Judges	1200–1020 BC	Judg	Israel is a loose confederacy of tribes united under the leadership of judges to defend against enemies.
United Monarchy	1020–922 BC	1 Sam–1 Kgs 11	Israel is governed by Kings Saul, David, and Solomon.
Divided Monarchy	922–597 BC	1 Kgs 12–2 Kgs	Israel, the northern kingdom, and Judah, the southern kingdom, are independently ruled.
Assyrian Siege	722 BC	2 Kgs 17	Israel falls to Assyria but Judah remains sovereign.
Babylonian Exile	(597) 586–539 BC	2 Kgs 25	Israel and Judah fall to Babylon and are systematically deported into exile.
Persian Liberation	539–333 BC	2 Chr 36:22-23, Ezra, Neh	Cyrus of Persia allows the exiles to return to Jerusalem.

- During what time period did the stories of 1 and 2 Samuel occur?
- During what time period were these stories recalled and recorded?
- How does the era of recollection affect our reading and interpretation of these stories?
- Why did the elders of Israel request a king?
- How would you describe the difference between the role of a judge and a king?
- What consequences would Israel endure if a king was appointed?
- How do you imagine Samuel felt at the end of 1 Samuel 8?
- How do you imagine his view of God and God's governance changed?

THE MEMORY

The Israelite people still had much to learn about God. In 597 BC, the Babylonians conquered northern Israel and began the deportation of Jews to Babylon. Those Jews residing in the southern kingdom (Judah) felt a sense of security due to their close proximity to the temple in Jerusalem. This was a false sense of security, however. In 586 BC, the Babylonians destroyed the temple in Jerusalem and began the deportation of the Judahites.

Israel's disobedience and rebellion caused these destructive days in Jewish history. Of course, not every Israelite taken into captivity could be considered rebellious. There were individuals like Daniel, Meshach, Shadrach, and Abednego who remained faithful even in captivity. There were prophets—Isaiah and Ezekiel—who continued to speak for God during these dark times. There were young children and no doubt others who remained faithful to God. And yet, all of these found themselves caught in a harsh political transition. They had been devoted, but now they were devastated.

The Israelite devastation was not just the result of being moved to Babylon. More devastating was the role of God in the transition. In Jeremiah 32, God acknowledges that he will "give [Jerusalem] into the hands of the Chaldeans and into the hand of Nebuchadrezzar of Babylon" (v. 28). By all indications, God had chosen Nebuchadrezzar as an instrument of divine will. The extent of this relationship cannot be understated. In Daniel 4, God relates to the Babylonian king in ways reflective of the divine relationship that existed between Israelite kings and God. God reveals truth to Nebuchadrezzar, provides prophets, rewards him, talks with him, and punishes him. God has adopted a foreigner as his instrument on earth. This shift was as devastating for the Israelite exile as the shift from theocracy to monarchy was for Samuel. It is easy to see why the Deuteronomic Historian chose to remember and relate Samuel's story to the captive population.

To make matters worse, the deliverer of the exiles, promised through the prophet Isaiah (Isaiah 40–55), would be a Persian king named Cyrus. In the past, Israel's deliverers had arisen from within the community of faith. They included people like Moses, Gideon, Deborah, Samson, and yes, even Samuel. This deliverer, who will be empowered by the Spirit of God (Isaiah 42:1), is from Persia. The exiled Israelites knew the tension of God's endorsement of alternative systems. In fact, the ancient transition from theocracy to monarchy probably seemed minor in comparison to God's blessing of a foreign system of government.

Experiencing the Broader Text

As the captive Jews struggled with their own past devotion and present devastation, these stories became their sources of hope. After reading these brief vignettes, respond to the questions that follow.

- 1 Samuel 1:1-20
- 1 Samuel 2:22–3:1
- 1 Samuel 4
- 1 Samuel 8

- How do you think the main character of each story feels about God?
- How might the exiled children of Israel have seen themselves in this story?
- What feelings and frustrations were similar?
- In what ways would this story define or provoke tension in the exile's life?
- Why did the Deuteronomic Historian include these stories as sources of hope for the exile?

Experiencing a Related Text

The Book of Daniel conveys stories that occurred during the Babylonian exile. Chapters 1–4 of Daniel contain stories specific to the relationship of King Nebuchadnezzar with Daniel and Daniel's God. It is evident from the text that God has chosen to engage in a relationship with Nebuchadnezzar. Read the texts listed below and answer the questions that follow.

- Daniel 2:46-49
- Daniel 3:28–4:3
- Daniel 4:29-37

- What confessions did Nebuchadnezzar make concerning the God of Israel?
- What events precipitated these confessions?
- How do we know God is interested in the life of Nebuchadnezzar?
- Is Nebuchadnezzar truly interested in the God of Israel?
- What would exiled Israelites infer from the apparent relationship between God and Nebuchadnezzar? How might they feel?
- How might Israelites assimilate those inferences into their belief system?

THE INTERPRETATION

Our modern society is no stranger to the political tensions of life. Our national history, faith history, and personal histories are marked with many milestones of transition. As a nation we have struggled through systemic changes in levels of freedom and responsibility. We have declared independence from a foreign, founding government. We have made the transition from a loose confederacy of colonies to a united national entity. We choose to operate within the tense rubric of a two-party system. We are familiar with the tension of politics.

The political tensions that are most prevalent in our lives, however, do not occur within the context of government. Our political tensions are the result of a more generic use of the word "politic"—competition between groups of individuals for power and leadership. These clashes occur within the more familiar arenas of our workplace, families, churches, and personal lives.

How do we survive these tensions? When a child who chooses to live by a different set of values challenges the system of family, how do we survive the tension? When churches go through systemic change in polity, doctrine, mission, or faith practice, how do we survive the tension? When the credibility of our personal values and beliefs is challenged, but changing them would incur some level of loss, how do we survive the tension? When we have been faithful and are committed to continued faithfulness, yet the culture and church are changing around us, how do we survive the tension?

First Samuel 8 and the surrounding stories from the life of Samuel give us hints for survival. This devoted judge was devastated by the political shifts that occurred during his day. But the record of his life provides thought-provoking truths—for exiled Israelites and for us.

- God cares for those who are devoted to the traditional systems of faith. God never abandoned Samuel.
- God does not abandon those who choose to live within an alternative expression of faith. God did not relate to the Israelites in the "same" way, but God never ceased relating to them.
- No system of faith perfectly reflects the will of God. While Samuel saw flaws within the monarchical system, there were obvious weaknesses in the human expression of the theocratic system as well. The determining factor for a system's success is whether God has supreme access to the system.
- It is not God's weakness, but rather God's grace, that prompts the divine embrace of our less than perfect systems.

Engaging Our Political Tensions

Having surveyed vignettes from 1 Samuel that illustrate the political tensions produced by shifts in faith and governmental systems, you are now ready to review areas where these tensions exist in your own life and history. Read the following sketches and answer the questions that follow.

Our National History

State Representatives arrived in Philadelphia on May 25, 1787, for the Constitutional Convention. These representatives from most of the thirteen original states met to revise the Articles of Confederation. Primarily successful farmers and businessmen, they felt that commerce and culture would thrive under a more centralized government, in comparison to their present loose confederation of states. The Constitution of the United States of America was birthed at this gathering.

Our Faith History
On October 31, 1517, Martin Luther nailed his 95 Theses against the sale of indulgences to the door of the Castle Church in Wittenberg. This date marks the traditional beginning of the Protestant Reformation.

Our Personal History
Within a traditional Baptist church in metropolitan Atlanta, three sets of parents have experienced the tension of systemic change based on the choices of their children. In one family, a son has embraced Roman Catholic beliefs and united his life with Benedictine monastery. In another family, a daughter has "come out of the closet" with regard to her sexuality and joined a downtown church that affirms God's presence and power in the lives of all Christians, regardless of their sexual preferences and predispositions. Other parents have struggled with their child marrying a person of another race.

- How would you describe person's devotions to the "old" systems in each of the above sketches?
- What difficulties or tensions were involved in understanding or embracing "new" systems?
- Where do the participants see God in each of these transitions?
- Where do you see God in each of these transitions?
- What moments in your life or the life of your church would be reflective of such transition and tension?
- Is it possible that God can be active in old and new systems? How?
- If the monarchy was not God's chosen will for Israel, yet God worked within it, can we assume that God can work within any system? Why or why not?

NOTES

¹ Eugene H. Peterson, *First and Second Samuel* (Louisville: Westminster/John Knox Press, 1999), 31-32.

² Bruce C. Birch, Walter Brueggemann, Terence E. Fretheim, David L. Petersen, *A Theological Introduction to the Old Testament* (Nashville: Abingdon Press, 1999), 216.

³ Walter Brueggemann, *First and Second Samuel*, Interpretation, A Bible Commentary for Teaching and Preaching (Louisville: John Knox Press, 1990), 63.

⁴ Ibid., 65.

⁵ Ibid., 63.

Chapter Two

SURVIVING THEOLOGICAL TENSION

SAUL: CHOSEN BUT CHASTISED

Focal Text: 1 Samuel 13:1-14   Broader Text: 1 Samuel 9–15

Within Israel's political tension, we have seen theocracy and monarchy serve as stereotypical extremes. These two governmental concepts could not be easily separated or sanctified. A careful reflection on the story of Samuel discloses that each was valuable to the purposes of God and neither was complete without some hint of the other. Theocracy hailed the God of Israel as its monarch and monarchy allowed the theocratic rule of God to choose Israel's kings. Samuel simply stood in the tension produced by these coexisting systems. He stood in the transitional moment between shifts in the dominance of a particular system.

These precepts are also true with regard to the theological concepts of law and grace. They are not easily separated or sanctified. Neither is complete without some hint of the other. Both are valuable to the purposes of God and coexist within the nature of God. And these are the stereotypical extremes that produce theological tension in the stories of Saul, our next focal character.

I'm convinced that one of the oldest tensions in existence is the tension between law and grace. This theological struggle emerged in the early chapters of human existence and continues to invade the human psyche today. In the beginning, God stated the law, "of the tree of the knowledge of good and evil you shall not eat, for in the day that you eat of it you shall die" (Gen 2:17). And in our fallenness, God opted for grace, "And the LORD God made garments of skins for the man and for his wife, and clothed them" (Gen 3:21).

It is not uncommon to hear parents who find themselves at the end of their rope exclaim, "If you can't live by my rules, then get out of my house!" And yet, when the bags are packed and sitting by the door, grace negotiates a settlement one more time. It is difficult to find a comfortable boundary between love and law. It is the supreme theological tension.

These extremes and their fuzzy boundary are often seen in God's self-disclosing moments. During the delivery of the Ten Commandments to Moses, God comments on the second command by saying, "I the LORD your God am a jealous God, punishing children for the iniquity of parents, to the third and the fourth generation of those who reject me, but showing steadfast love to the thousandth generation of those who love me and keep my commandments" (Exod 20:5-6). This same self-disclosed tension is recorded in Exodus 34:6-7. When God speaks about God's self, ambiguity and tension are confessed. The boundary between law and grace is even difficult for God to manage. Like a divine parent, at different moments and in different eras, God's nature is slanted toward one extreme or the other.

Saul, the first king of Israel, is a pivotal character in this theological tension. He stands between two theological covenants that competitively coexsist and represent the legal and loving tensions within the heart of God. The covenant within which Saul experienced and expressed faith was the Mosaic covenant. This covenant is recorded in Exodus 19:5. God communicates with Israel through Moses, saying, "if you obey my voice and keep my covenant, you shall be my treasured possession out of all the peoples." While this conditional statement certainly carries elements of relationship within its linguistic structure, it is primarily defined by law. Obedience was the key to relationship.

In comparison, the Davidic covenant was primarily relational in language and nature. The words of this covenant are recorded in 2 Samuel 7:12-16. In this text, God promises David through the prophet Nathan, "I will raise up your offspring after you . . . . I will establish the throne of his kingdom forever . . . . When he commits iniquity, I will punish him . . . . But I will not take my steadfast love from him, as I took it from Saul." While the legal aspect of this covenant is evident, it does not take precedence over the relational aspect of the covenant. Steadfast love is the primary key to this relationship. In fact, God acknowledges that there is a difference in the covenantal relationship experienced by Saul and the covenantal relationship of those who will rule after him. Saul lived under a covenant in which God's love was "more conditional" than the covenant experienced by David and his offspring.

Saul sits on the fateful bridge that moves Israel from a covenant relationship dominated by justice to a covenant relationship dominated by grace. On the one hand, Saul, like David, enjoys the privilege of being chosen. But on the other hand, Saul will reign and be chastised under the justice of the Mosaic covenant. David will not endure such a fate.

THE OCCURRENCE

It was 9:00 AM on a mid-September Monday. The bell had rung, my fellow students were seated, and the teacher stood facing us with a stack of papers in her hands. I had taken my first algebra exam three days prior to this morning. Ms. Duncan had graded them over the weekend and the fateful day of their return had arrived. She walked around the room, calling our names and distributing the documents into trembling hands. Smiles and winces erupted on the faces of my classmates. I winced—a 79. It wasn't the first C of my academic career. It wasn't the worst grade of my academic career. It was, however, indicative of my subsequent struggles through the world of algebra. (I much preferred Ms. Finley's creative writing class.)

First Samuel 13:1-14 is not the most tragic of Saul's blunders. Nor is it a climactic blunder in the scope of his story. First Samuel 13 is our focal text because it is the beginning of Saul's spiral away from the favor of God. It is indicative of his subsequent struggles in the pioneering role of king.

1 Samuel 13:1. Our text begins in v. 1 with a sketchy reference to Saul's age and time in office. In many ways, the language and structure of this verse is not unlike other chronological references used by the Deuteronomic Historian in 1 and 2 Kings. It is unique, however, in that it is incomplete. In the Hebrew text, Saul's actual age is not included and there is even some question concerning the accuracy of the length of his reign.[1] Could the dubious recollection of Saul's early years be a subconscious statement about the efficiency of his regal era?

1 Samuel 13:2-5. As uncertain as the text seems to be concerning Saul's age and years of reign, the same uncertainty exists with regard to locations. In vv. 2-5, the details of our text get more confusing with references to Jonathan's presence at both Gebeah and Geba. The Hebrew root of these place names means "hill." Many Palestinian cities were named according to geographic features that existed near their location. With numerous ancient Palestinian towns located near hills, scholars have found it difficult to know exactly which town or towns are meant by the text.

Former pastor and present scholar Eugene Peterson has suggested that the narrator's mention of chronological and geographical references has little to do with the intent of the text. These years and place names, as well as subsequent troop movements and battle terrain, are provided to insure the reader that Saul's faith was tested in the real world.[2] Saul is not a mythological being fighting mean pirates in Neverland. He is real. His world is real. The Philistines are dangerously real. And the challenges of faith are real.

1 Samuel 13:6-8. In vv. 6-7, we find Saul serving as the military leader of fearful but faithful Israelites. Saul's warriors hide and hover under the leadership of Saul. They are far outnumbered, but Saul is God's chosen warrior.

Philistine Chariot
(Illustration Credit: Barclay Burns)

After seven days of avoiding their enemy, however, morale began to wane. According to v. 8, God's other chosen warrior, Samuel, was to arrive within a seven-day window and ceremonially prepare the troops for battle. This is the same Samuel who handily subdued the Philistines in chapter 7. With Saul and Samuel together, this smattering of soldiers had all the divine assurance for victory that they needed. At the end of seven days, however, Samuel had not arrived and the soldiers began to "slip away from Saul" (v. 8).

1 Samuel 13:9. In an effort to maintain troop loyalty and appease the ritual demands of God, Saul assumed a priestly role and decided to present a burnt offering and peace offering to God. The burnt offering was a means of purification and the peace offering promoted a sense of unity with God.[3] Both of these elements were essential in Israel's preparation for war.

Some readers of the text are quick to label Saul disobedient and irreverent for performing this sacred, priestly ritual. They see his embrace of the priestly role as an indication he has disregarded or forgotten the precepts and presence of

God.⁴ But is that conclusion consistent with the text? It appears that Saul made a sound and valid decision.⁵ Saul does not hastily offer the sacrifice. His wait for Samuel is well documented in the text. And the fact that Saul sacrifices to God is a testimony to his regard for the necessity of the ritual and God's ensuing presence. Saul has not lost regard for God. Rather, he seems to act out of deep respect and reverence for God.

1 Samuel 13:10-14. Verse 10 indicates that Samuel arrived as soon as Saul had finished the ritual of the burnt offering. Whatever confrontation Saul had expected with the Philistines, I'm sure it paled in comparison to the reception he received from Samuel. Saul moved toward the arriving Samuel in order to bless (salute) him; Samuel, on the other hand, intended to bless Saul out!

In v. 11, Samuel questions Saul's actions and Saul responds with reasonable explanations. Samuel ignores the possible validity of Saul's acts and proceeds to levy accusations and judgments against him in v. 13. Samuel's anger, however, appears to lack any real basis. Samuel mentions "the commandment of the LORD" that has been broken, yet Samuel cites no commandment and it is impossible to construe one from prior biblical texts. If this act was an illegal intrusion into the priestly role, then David and Solomon would later be guilty of the same intrusion, but with no admonitions. In fact, their sacrifices will be found acceptable (2 Sam 6:17f; 24:25; 1 Kgs 3:3f).⁶

Samuel's reprimand also raises the issue of Saul's kingdom legacy in vv. 13b-14. Stripping Saul of this future honor makes little logical sense, however. In the first place, Saul apparently has not been informed of this eternal opportunity. And second, the narrative does not indicate he was ever informed that the inappropriate offering of particular sacrifices was a condition of this kingdom promise.⁷ Adding to the illogical nature of this portion of Samuel's tirade is the mention of the appointment of the king who is to succeed Saul. On the one hand, it is stated that the king has been chosen on the basis of Saul's sacrificial infraction. On the other hand, it appears the appointment was a completed deal before the infraction. This would suggest that the continuance of Saul's kingdom was never a real possibility.

The most illogical facet of Samuel's speech, however, has little to do with words and much to do with timing. Remember, *Samuel* is late for the sacrifice. It was Samuel who did not meet the deadline for preparing God's army for war. The one agreement to which we are privy within the text is the designated window of opportunity for preparation. It is Samuel who scurries in after the deadline and expects to be forgiven for his disregard and disobedience. The priest wishes to live according to grace while he expects the king to live according to law. This is the tension that defines Saul's reign. The deck is stacked against Saul, Samuel is dealing, and the next king will get the better hand . . . and the more graceful covenant.

When Our Best Is Not Enough

In a book titled *Shame and Grace*, Lewis Smedes, a professor of psychology at Fuller Theological Seminary, addresses the seemingly universal struggle with shame. He pinpoints three sources from which this burden arises: the secular culture that attempts to define how a person should look and feel, unaccepting parents who convince us we will never live up to their expectations, and religious institutions that instruct us to follow rules explicitly or face eternal punishment.[8] Even at our best, none of us are able to live up to the expectations these arenas of influence place upon us. As humans, our best never seems to be enough.

The same was true for Saul. Review the focal text in light of the challenges listed below. Then answer the questions provided for reflection.

(1) Saul faced the challenge of the throne. (1 Sam 13:1)
(2) Saul faced the challenge of military leadership. (1 Sam 13:2-4)
(3) Saul faced the challenge of protecting his people. (1 Sam 13:5-7)
(4) Saul faced the challenge of patience. (1 Sam 13:8)
(5) Saul faced the challenge of faith practice. (1 Sam 13:9-10)
(6) Saul received the criticism of Samuel. (1 Sam 13:11-14)

- How well do you feel Saul endured the challenges set before him?
- How would you have responded to these challenges differently?
- How do you feel about Samuel's reaction to Saul's attempts at leadership?
- What kind of realistic or unrealistic expectations were placed on Saul by culture, family, and religion?
- How do you think God felt about Saul's sacrifice?
- Was Saul's experience weighted toward law or grace?

Fulfilling the Role

Serving as the first king of Israel placed Saul in a position of definition. How he served and the roles he played in the life of the nation would set a standard to be followed or adjusted by those who came after him. Such is the case with most pioneer efforts.

Review the focal text again, giving attention to the various roles embodied by Saul. Then answer the questions that follow.

(1) Saul the King (v. 1)
(2) Saul the Military Leader (vv. 2-4)
(3) Saul the Pastor (vv. 5-7)
(4) Saul the Priest (vv. 8-10)
(5) Saul the Human (vv. 11-14)

1 Samuel 9:26-27—Samuel anoints Saul as king. Samuel first anointed Saul in a private ceremony outside an unnamed city in the "land of Zuph."

Julius Schnoor von Carolsfeld. *Samuel Anoints Saul as King*. 19th century. Woodcut. *Das Buch der Bucher in Bilden*. (Credit: Dover Pictorial Archive Series)

- Were these valid roles for Saul to fill? Why or why not?
- What strengths and weaknesses did he display within each role?
- How might he have functioned within the role differently?
- How do you think God felt about Saul's performance in these roles?

THE MEMORY

Of the primary human characters in 1 and 2 Samuel (Samuel, Saul, and David), it may be Saul with whom the exiled Israelites could best relate. Saul was chosen; Israel was chosen. Saul was subject to the ambiguous sermons of a prophet; Israel had her prophets as well. Saul was stuck between law and grace; Israel found herself in the same tight spot.

Outside 1 Samuel 13, the broader text of Saul's life further reflects this tension between law and grace. Saul is truly, gracefully chosen, yet he is held accountable to Mosaic law. In chapters 9–11 of 1 Samuel, the reader is provided a vivid view of Saul's chosenness. In 1 Samuel 9, Samuel is instructed to find the new king who will save the Israelites from the Philistines. There is no doubt God is directly involved in the choosing of this new leader in Israel.

In 1 Samuel 10, Samuel anoints Saul. The anointing was a symbolic expression of the conveyance of God's blessing on Saul. This chapter does not end with symbolism, however. Verse 10 records a more literal episode of God's conveyance of power and presence. Saul meets a

Saul's Activities
In considering the length of Saul's reign, it is helpful to review the major events of his life, as recorded in 1 Samuel:

1. Saul seeks lost donkeys and finds a kingdom (9:1–10:16).
2. Saul is chosen by lottery at Mizpah (10:17-27).
3. Saul rouses Israel, defeats the Ammonites, and is confirmed as king (11:1-15).
4. Saul and Jonathan lead Israel against the Philistines (13:1–14:52).
5. Saul defeats the Amalekites, but angers Samuel (15:1-35).
6. Saul suffers from an evil spirit and is comforted by David's music (16:14-23).
7. Saul faces the Philistines, but David fights Goliath (17:1-58).
8. Saul grows jealous of David and tries to kill him (18–20).
9. Saul hunts David: several encounters (21–26).
10. Saul seeks advice from Samuel's ghost before battling the Philistines (28).
11. Saul and three of his sons die in battle with the Philistines (31).

Jonathan the Brave
(Illustration Credit: Barclay Burns)

band of prophets on the road to Gibeah and the Spirit of God possesses him.

Finally, in 1 Samuel 11, Saul leads an attack against the Ammonites raiding Jabesh-Gilead. In v. 6, Saul is empowered by the Spirit of God and achieves a great military victory. In light of his success, it is Samuel who suggests a celebration and reaffirmation of Saul's kingship! Saul is chosen, filled, and empowered by the Spirit of God. Prophet and people recognize him as God's leader. But he will not retain this blessed status.

In 1 Samuel 13, Saul engages the wrath of Samuel that we have previously discussed. In chapter 14, he makes rash oaths that endanger the lives of his son Jonathan and soldiers. And in chapter 15, he willfully disobeys God's commands concerning the complete slaughter of the Amalekites. By the end of chapter 15, God is sorry Saul was appointed king. The chapter concludes with a sense of separation; Samuel separated himself from Saul and the reader senses that God has stepped away as well. In 1 Samuel 16:1, God instructs Samuel to anoint a new king.

The themes that pervade the story of Saul were far too familiar to the exiled Israelites in Babylon. They had known the blessings of chosenness. They had made mistakes—some purposeful and some understood only in the mysterious minds of their prophets. They were now experiencing separation. And it seemed that a new king, maybe even a new nation, had been chosen to replace them.

The theological tension that emerges from the exilic experience is obvious. The Israelites were captives in Babylon. The chosen nation, which had enjoyed God's promise of steadfast love and mercy, found a boundary to eternal love and mercy. This population, who had taken for granted the grace of the Davidic covenant, found themselves judged by Mosaic standards. The chosen people had become a chastised people who could only repent . . . and hope.

Relating to Saul

As previously stated, Saul may be the character in the Deuteronomic History with whom the exiled Israelites most easily identified. While Samuel seems to do no wrong, and David will do wrong and yet be forgiven, Saul's life is a down-to-earth mix of emotions and decisions for which he is fatefully held responsible. He will accept God's call to be king, he will be chastised for his failure to execute the role properly, and he will eventually reign in the shadow of another chosen to replace him. This is a chronology with which Israel can relate. The exiles had been God's chosen people, were being chastised for not executing that role properly, and seemed to exist in the shadow of a foreign government ordained by their God.

Review the following outline of Saul's life. The literary structure presented by the Deuteronomic Historian vividly accentuates this chronology: a positive ascent, a negative decline, and an eventual secondary role. Answer the questions that follow.

I. The Positive Ascent of Saul
   A. Saul is chosen by God. (1 Sam 9)
   B. Saul is anointed by God. (1 Sam 10)
   C. Saul is empowered by God. (1 Sam 11)

II. The Demise of Saul
   A. An inappropriate sacrifice at Gilgal (1 Sam 13)
   B. An inappropriate oath in Ephraim (1 Sam 14)
   C. An inappropriate sparing of Agag (1 Sam 15)

III. The Secondary Role of Saul
   A. Saul is comforted by David. (1 Sam 16)
   B. Saul is defended by David. (1 Sam 17)
   C. Saul is jealous of David. (1 Sam 18–20)
   D. Saul pursues David. (1 Sam 21–26)
   E. Saul's death grieves David. (1 Sam 31)

- In what ways might exiled Israelites see themselves in the cycle of Saul's story? What incidents in their history would be interpreted as "ascents" and "demises"?
- How would their situation differ from the struggles of Saul?
- How might the exiled Israelites reconcile their experience of both the Mosaic and Davidic covenants?
- Did they deserve the legal consequences of the Mosaic covenant? Why?
- Was the Davidic covenant a source of hope for them? Why?
- From which covenant do you think an exilic prophet might preach? Why?

THE INTERPRETATION

Saul's fateful existence within the tension of law and grace is not unique. The exiles of Israel could easily relate to the confusion of trusting God's grace and at the same time needing to give full attention to God's law. We know this tension as well.

Every person of faith lives with a similar internal struggle. Some are more weighted toward Mosaic covenant. They carry a burden of guilt and shame that arises from their humanity, preventing their attainment of holiness. Others live weighted toward the Davidic covenant. They embrace a twisted confidence in the grace of God. Because they have chosen God (and feel that God has chosen them) their actions take a backseat to the fervency of belief. They are "sure" they are saved, certain they are forgiven of all sins—past, present, and future—so they live with less regard for the laws of God.

Within this tension, the role of the prophet is tricky. The prophet must assess which covenant we tend to lean toward. The prophet must challenge that covenant with the alternative covenant. And yet, the prophet must maintain that both covenants are a vital part of the nature of God and faith. When we rest too secure in the Davidic promise, the prophet must challenge us with law. When we are guilt-ridden over our shortcomings under the Mosaic Law, the prophet must remind us of God's everlasting love and mercy.

In the process, we learn that God's nature truly embraces both covenants. God endures the tension for our benefit. Our faith must be lived in the theological tension that exists between these two covenants—between law and grace.

Engaging Theological Tension

The following readings are provided to help you engage the theological tension that exists between law and grace. The first reading addresses the tension as it exists within the nature of God, the second as it exists within the nature of humanity, and the third as it exists within the nature of the church.

Reading #1—Exodus 34:6-8

Reading #2—A college professor attempted to resolve the tension between law and grace by telling his class, "We must work as if salvation completely depends upon us, but trust that salvation completely depends upon God."

Reading #3—Recently I have been asking a question of strangers—for example, seatmates on an airplane—when I strike up a conversation. "When I say the words 'evangelical Christian' what comes to mind?" In reply, mostly I hear political descriptions: of strident pro-life activists, or gay-rights opponents, or proposals for censoring the Internet . . . Not once—*not once*—have I heard a description redolent of grace. Apparently that is not the aroma Christians give off in the world.[9]

- Does it surprise you that theological tension exists in the life of God? Why or why not?
- Do you expect to see the same tension in the realms of humanity and the church?
- What contradictions and struggles do the above readings present?
- How have you experienced these tensions, struggles, and contradictions in your life? As a parent? As a child? As an employee? As a church member?
- Is your life weighted toward law or grace? Your family? Your friends? Your church?

NOTES

[1] Ralph W. Klein, *I Samuel*, Word Biblical Commentary (Waco: Word, Incorporated, 1993), 124.

[2] Eugene H. Peterson, *First and Second Samuel* (Louisville: Westminster/John Knox Press, 1999), 79.

[3] Tony W. Cartledge, *I & II Samuel*, Smyth and Helwys Bible Commentary (Macon: Smyth and Helwys Publishing, Inc., 2001), 172.

[4] Peterson, 79.

[5] John Claypool, *Glad Reunion, Meeting Ourselves in the Lives of Bible Men and Women* (Waco: Word Incorporated, 1985), 85.

[6] R. P. Gordon, *1 & 2 Samuel* (Sheffield England: Sheffield Academic Press, 1984), 55.

[7] Walter Brueggemann, *First and Second Samuel*, Interpretation, A Bible Commentary for Teaching and Preaching (Louisville: John Knox Press, 1990), 101.

[8] Philip Yancey, *What's So Amazing about Grace?* (Grand Rapids: Zondervan Publishing House, 1997), 36.

[9] Ibid., 31.

Chapter Three

SURVIVING RELATIONAL TENSION

DAVID: WEAK BUT WINNING

Focal Text: 1 Samuel 16:1-13   Broader Text: 1 Samuel 16–2 Samuel 24

We live in a competitive world. Regardless of our daily contexts, we contend with situations and individuals that expose our weaknesses. At times, we can conceal these weaknesses. At other times, they are quite conspicuous. Once revealed, they often become the basis of our being chosen or, more often, overlooked for particular tasks.

I endured that torture many times during my childhood. My small frame, short stature, and late growth spurt left me vulnerable to the strengths of other children my age. As is common on most playgrounds and in most backyards, we would gather for athletic events. Captains would be appointed (usually self-appointed) and the choosing of teams would commence. My only hope of not being chosen last was if Kenneth Baxter, my best friend, was a captain. Even then, there were days when he couldn't sacrifice the win for my weakness.

Weakness is always relative. People are only weak in comparison to others who are stronger. If an individual existed alone, the idea of weak and strong would not exist. It is because we are relational creatures that the idea of competitive weakness and strength subsist. This is a relational tension.

The "selection process" further heightens this tension. If the strong were always chosen and always won, the tension would be minimal. Pecking orders would be established, outcomes could be easily predicted, and our primary tension would be internal. We would wish to be stronger, struggle to be stronger, and maybe even despise those who were stronger. But only those who found themselves to be relatively weak would experience this type of tension. The introduction of the selection process, however, opens new possibilities and creates an element of tension for everyone. The weak might be chosen. The weak might be on the team that wins. Within a relational system that depends upon a selection process, the possibilities are endless. This creates tension . . . even for the powerful.

As stated in the previous chapter, Saul was perhaps the one character in the Deuteronomic History with whom Israel could most easily identify. David, however, is the most popular and familiar character of 1 and 2 Samuel. This is not because we so easily identify with David, but rather because we would *like* to identify with him. David is the quintessential underdog able to overcome. David appears to be weak, yet he is chosen in the selection process. David is a winner. He personifies who we wish to be and who the exiled Israelites longed to be.

To be chosen by God places even the weakest individual in a position to win. It also places the powerful in a vulnerable situation; relational tension is created. This mysteriously unpredictable God of Israel often operates as a friend. Like a Kenneth Baxter of the cosmos, God often chooses the weaker on the basis of relationship rather than inherent strength. God will choose those whose hearts are well developed rather than their muscles or even their minds. In fact, this unpredictable God almost predictably chooses the unexpected, weaker individuals to carry the ball.

THE OCCURRENCE

As we will later see, any story from the life of David would adequately illustrate his survival of relational tension. Almost every Davidic story recorded by the Deuteronomic Historian contains some element of tension between the weak and the strong. David's humble beginning, however, may best illustrate the point and provide a basis for understanding the chapters of his life that follow.

1 Samuel 16:1-2. In 16:1, the tension is obvious. In fact, this may be one of the tensest moments in Old Testament Scripture. Within the parameters of one verse, all four primary characters of 1 and 2 Samuel are present or alluded to:

God, Samuel, Saul, and David. The reader immediately gets the sense that something pivotal and provocative will soon occur.

It is difficult, however, to determine who is weak and who is strong in this text. Samuel, the once strong and fiery prophet, now grieves and fears Saul. Saul, the military strategist, is assumed to be easily misled by a divinely inspired lie. And of course, there is the issue of the divine lie. If God is all-powerful and able to protect Samuel, why concoct a tale concerning his presence in Bethlehem?

Bethlehem adds to the relational tension as well. The new king's city of origin is not one of the power bases of the ancient world. Bethlehem was outside the governed territories of Saul and it was not a part of the usual route of Samuel's influence.[1] This small village was not the obvious birthplace of a king. It was a weak place that secretly held the anointed of God—a heritage that would continue until the birth of the Messiah.

1 Samuel 16:4-5. Although Samuel's "sacrificial excuse" was apparently adequate in distracting Saul, it did not diminish the elders' fear. In v. 4, the elders come trembling to meet Samuel and question his intentions. The elders of a town were typically the oldest and wisest of the local population. They regularly met at the city gate to settle disputes, enforce law, and serve as witnesses to various types of business transactions.[2] They recognized Samuel and immediately became fearful. They held the governing

Michelangelo's *David*
The most famous image in our world of the figure of David is this colossal sculpture by Michelangelo. The contemplative David sees Goliath in the distance and concentrates on the action about to happen. The strain of this event is seen only in the muscles of his neck and his knitted brow. His body is depicted in the relaxed position known as contrapposto that was used in 5th century Classic Greek sculpture.

Michelangelo (1475–1564). *David*. 1502-04. Marble. 14'1".Museo di Accademia del Disegno, Florence, Italy. (Credit: Planet Art)

powers of their locale, yet they felt weak in Samuel's presence. Weakness is always relative.

Samuel assures the elders of his peaceful intentions, but the reader doubts they are truly satisfied. They probably eyed Samuel with the same curious suspicion with which townsfolk of the old American West eyed gunfighters when they rode into town. The gunfighter might say he is "just passing through," but the six-shooter on his hip said otherwise. Samuel doesn't carry a six-shooter; he carries a ram's horn filled with oil. The last time the elders saw that horn of oil was right after they requested their first king. It was the horn of oil used at the anointing of Saul. Samuel carries the horn again; something is about to happen.

1 Samuel 16:6-12. Verses 6-12 contain the climax toward which these earlier hints of relational tension have been moving. Jesse's sons are paraded before Samuel. Within the story, it appears that only Samuel knows the purpose of this pageant and only Samuel hears the urgings of God.

When Eliab passed before Samuel, the purposeful prophet is immediately enamored with his strength and stature. God advises against Eliab as well as the method of "visual selection" Samuel employed. After all, Saul was "head and shoulders taller" than any man (1 Sam 10:23), but his physical characteristics had not proved to be adequate qualifications for royalty. The Lord was searching for someone with a particular heart.

Six more sons of Jesse pass before Samuel, but the prophet feels no divine inclination toward selection. Sure of his mission but unsure of the reason for God's silence, Samuel finally asks, "Are all your sons here?" (1 Sam 16:11). According to Jesse, one son remains. But in the mind of Jesse (and probably in the minds of everyone else in the room) the remaining child was the least expected choice. On the playground of faith, however, this child had caught the eye of God.

Finally, the child enters. Although we have been informed that appearance matters little, the narrator is immediately struck by the child's physical characteristics. His skin, his eyes, his total persona were too striking to ignore. The voice of God once again rings in Samuel's ear, "this is the one" (1 Sam 16:12).

In v. 13, Samuel anoints David with oil. This ritual was a symbolic expression of God's blessing upon the anointed. In David's life, however, this symbol pointed toward a powerful reality. The narrator wishes the reader to know that the Spirit of the Lord came upon David at his anointing and stayed upon David throughout his life. This was in direct contrast to the Spirit's activity in the life of Saul. Saul was empowered by God's Spirit during a confrontation with prophets sometime after his anointing. There was also no sense of permanence in Saul's experience of the Spirit—it came and went. David's reception of God's Spirit was immediate and permanent.[3]

1 Samuel 16—Carolsfeld has captured Jesse's surprise at learning that God had chosen David, rather than one of his older sons, to be king.

Julius Schnoor von Carolsfeld. *David Is Anointed King.* 19th century. Woodcut. *Das Buch der Bucher in Bilden.* (Credit: Dover Pictorial Archive Series)

From the very beginning of David's saga, we see perceived weakness evolve into strength. Being chosen and empowered by God makes success a possibility in the life of Jesse's youngest and weakest son. The same is true for the exiled Israelites . . . and for us.

Power Assessments

In the family movie *Hook*, Dustin Hoffman plays Captain Hook, the villainous rival of the grown-up Peter Pan, played by Robin Williams. Captain Hook sees himself as a debonair and ageless icon. The Lost Boys see him as a pirate to be feared or fought. His fellow pirates see him as a role model to be emulated. Peter Pan sees him as a providentially defeated adversary. The child heroine of the movie sees him as "a mean old man who needs a mommy."

Weakness is always relative. We define our strengths and weaknesses by the perceived strengths and weaknesses of those with whom we are in contact.

Answer the following questions with regard to the characters in the focal text.

- Is Saul a strong or weak character? Who perceived him as strong and who perceived him as weak? How did Saul perceive himself?
- Was Samuel a strong or weak character? Who perceived him as strong and who perceived him as weak? How did Samuel perceive himself?

- Were the elders strong or weak characters? Who perceived them as strong and who perceived them as weak? How did they perceive themselves?
- Was Jesse a strong or weak character? Who perceived him as strong and who perceived him as weak? How did he perceive himself?
- Were Eliab and Abinadab strong or weak characters? Who perceived them as strong and who perceived them as weak? How did they perceive themselves?
- Was David a strong or weak character? Who perceived him as strong and who perceived him as weak? How did he perceive himself?
- Was God a strong or weak character? Who perceived God as strong and who perceived God as weak? What was God's self-perception?

THE MEMORY

Although David's humble beginnings are vivid indications of the relational tension present in his life, the breadth of his story demands we look at other episodes as well. Since forty of the fifty-five chapters of 1 and 2 Samuel record incidents from the life of David, it is clear that the Deuteronomic Historian felt the Davidic saga would be a primary source of hope for the exiled Israelites.

At times, the saga exposes David's struggles with his own weaknesses. At other times, it allows us to observe David's stronger role as he responds to the weaknesses of others. And while we cannot address every narrative within the confines of this study, we can meander among these moments of weakness and strength that give rise to David's relational tension. As we watch the Davidic story move beyond our focal text, it will be easy to observe the continued development of this relational tension.

From the beginning, we have seen the inherent relative weakness of David. Within the verses of 1 Samuel 16–17, David is portrayed as a shepherd boy, a young musician, and an unknown warrior. These images did not cause his father or his brothers to think of him as powerful, royal material. These images were also inconsistent with the characteristics possessed by the judges (and king) who preceded David. Saul, as well as his judicial predecessors, was of great stature and had a commanding charisma. This was apparently not the case with David.

Though none of David's early portraits portrayed him as powerful, this young man seemed to be a winner nonetheless. The shepherd boy treated as a virtual nonentity in the family of Jesse was anointed king.[4] The young musician is the only person able to soothe the reigning king. And the unknown warrior wreaks havoc on the Philistines and their prized giant, Goliath. In these earliest chapters, David is a marginal character who is uncredentialed and has no real social stature.[5] And yet, David always manages to win.

Some of the weaknesses in David's life had nothing to do with credentials or social status, however. Like most of us, many of his weaknesses were the result of circumstance and choice. The circumstances created by David's youthful successes at war produced a deep jealousy within the heart of King Saul. This generated a period of weakness in David's life that is recorded in 1 Samuel 18–28.

In chapters 18–20, David must be protected from Saul by Jonathan, Saul's son. Jonathan's relationship with his father, though at times estranged, made him privy to some of his father's harmful plans with regard to David. Jonathan is consistent in his care of David and his warnings to him.

In chapters 21–22, we find David harbored and protected by the priests of Nob. Saul's obsessive anger toward David reached the point that David had to flee Saul's presence. He was fed by the priests of Nob and secretly sent on his way. Upon entering the city of Gath, he was recognized as the great warrior and future king of Israel. Fearing that the local king, Achish, might plan ill against him, David feigned madness and escaped. Finally, in chapter 22, David is hiding in a cave in Adullam and the priests of Nob are being slaughtered for harboring him earlier. This series of episodes paint a picture of a weak but resourceful David; he knows how to survive.

The next series of stories that display David's weaknesses begins in 2 Samuel 11. In chapter 11, the Deuteronomic Historian records David's affair with Bathsheba and the murderous drama that follows. David chose to commit adultery with Bathsheba and then learned that she was pregnant with his child. In an attempt to cover his sin, David devised several plots involving her husband, Uriah the Hittite. David first called Uriah home from the battlefield and tried to encourage him to spend time with and sleep with his wife, Bathsheba. When the child was born, Uriah would then think it was his own. Uriah's devotion to his military comrades and the Lord's cause, however, prevented Uriah from sharing this intimacy with his wife. David got Uriah drunk, hoping the

This illustration imagines that David was playing the harp, rather than napping, prior to his encounter with Bathsheba.

Julius Schnoor von Carolsfeld. *David and Bathsheba*. 19th century. Woodcut. *Das Buch der Bucher in Bilden*. (Credit: Dover Pictorial Archive Series)

intoxication might weaken his ethic. Still Uriah refrained from sexual pleasure while the Lord's army was fighting elsewhere. (With regard to strength and weakness, it is interesting to note that the foreign Hittite shows more strength with regard to God's law than the chosen King of Israel.)

Finally, realizing the strength of Uriah's conscience, David devised a plot to have Uriah killed. After Uriah's death, David was able to take Bathsheba as his wife, allow her to bear the child, and safeguard his adulterous affair—or so he thought.

Before the birth of the child, the prophet Nathan parabolically confronts David and David unknowingly pronounces his own sentence—death (2 Sam 12:5). Nathan informs David that "the LORD has put away your sin; you shall not die" (2 Sam 12:13). But death is the verdict for the firstborn son of David and Bathsheba. Amid all this grief, however, the savvy reader is aware that Bathsheba will bear another child, Solomon, and he will reign as the next King of Israel. And the savvy Christian is aware that Bathesheba, the wife of Uriah, has become a part of the lineage of Jesus the Messiah (Matt 1:6). God takes the worst of our weaknesses and works them for his good.

Following the child's death, violence never seems to leave the house of David. Second Samuel 13–20 is a painful succession of weak moments in the lives of David and his family. Amnon, David's oldest son, rapes his half-sister Tamar. Absalom, Tamar's brother, kills Amnon in revenge. Though Absalom is later restored to the family (after a period of banishment) bitterness has infiltrated the family system. Eventually, Absalom leads a revolt against his father, David. When the rebellion ends, Absalom is dead at the hands of Joab, David's trusted general. A grief-stricken and aged David is barely able to keep his mind on the affairs of the kingdom in chapter 19.

Before this series of painful events ends, David must attempt to muster the strength to squash a revolt and fight another giant. Yes . . . just as his story began with a giant, it also moves toward its conclusion with a giant. In 2 Samuel 22:15-17, David's life has come full circle. He is again at war with the Philistines and they have once again presented a giant as their prized warrior. His name is Ishbibenob. During this battle, however, David does not pick up a handful of smooth stones, swing a sling, and enjoy a God-given victory. Rather, David is so wearied in the battle that his fellow soldiers must rescue him. They kill the giant for him and demand that he refrain from engaging in Israel's battles. David is weak, but he still survives; he still wins through the care of his friends.

It would not be fair or accurate only to highlight David's weaknesses within the relational tensions of his life. After all, David was the King of Israel. And on numerous occasions he was the stronger entity within the relational tensions of his life. Others were usually perceived as weak in comparison to David, and it was his ability to exercise vulnerability and empathy that made him a memorable hero.

David's story vividly details his compassion for and emotional understanding of those who were suffering. It was a part of David's magnetism to attract the political and economic outcasts of Israel.[6] In 1 Samuel 18, David forges a deep friendship with Jonathan, the son of King Saul. Although, as we have previously observed, Jonathan is often the protector of David, David is also keenly aware of the weak moment Jonathan endures. After all, Jonathan is the king's son. Jonathan is the logical heir to the throne. And yet, it is David who has been chosen and anointed. David affords the politically lame young man a unique and compassionate friendship.

Even during the time that David lives his life as a fugitive, weak in relation to King Saul, he is sensitive to the needs of those who are relatively weaker. In 1 Samuel 22, David hides from Saul in the cave of Adullam. Word of his whereabouts spreads quickly through the impoverished corners of Saul's kingdom and v. 2 records, "Everyone who was in distress, and everyone who was in debt, and everyone who was discontented gathered to him."

In 1 Samuel 25, David's wandering group of vagabonds approaches the home of a man named Nabal. Nabal is described in the text as "surly and mean" (25:3). It is no surprise that Nabal ridicules and refuses to aid David and his entourage. In retaliation for Nabal's lack of hospitality, David plans an attack on Nabal's home. Abigail, Nabal's wife, learns of David's plans. She brings provisions and gifts to David in an effort to redeem the ill done by her belligerent husband. Swayed by her humble plea, David grants her request for safety. (Ten days later, the Lord struck Nabal dead.) There is no doubt that David has a heart for those who are weak.

Probably the most unique aspect of David's empathy was his ability to understand, or at least tolerate, the weakness that existed in the hearts of the powerful. David's refusal to relinquish his loyalty to and affection for Saul cannot be overlooked. While being pursued by Saul, David twice had opportunity to kill him but would not (1 Sam 24 and 26). And at Saul's death, David and all the men who were with him "mourned and wept, and fasted until evening" (2 Sam 1:12). David conducted himself impeccably as he awaited the throne.[7] He understood and endured the weaknesses that existed in people of power. He realized that the "up and in" needed God's grace as desperately as the "down and out." The stories of this weak and wonderful hero had much to convey to a nation in Babylonian exile.

David was a survivor. As a vulnerable young warrior, he survived. As a fugitive, in the cross hairs of Saul's jealous wrath, he survived. He survived the death of a child, the death of a friendship, the death of a friend, and the rebellion and death of a second child. He survived war and famine and grief. He just found a way to survive . . . and to help others survive.

It is no wonder that the story of David dominates the Deuteronomic Historian's record. The exiles needed to know that they were still God's chosen children. The exiles needed to know that, even in their weakest moments, God's presence and providence were still on their side. The exiles needed to be reminded of the steadfast love and mercy promised to David. The exiles needed just enough hope to survive . . . and to help others survive.

The Best of Times and the Worst of Times

The best and worst times of David's life spoke volumes to the exiled Israelites who remembered his stories. Read the following narratives from the menagerie of Davidic memories. Then, answer the questions listed with regard to each story.

1 Samuel 16:1-13
1 Samuel 17:31-49
1 Samuel 18:1-12

1 Samuel 24:1-17
2 Samuel 7:12-17
2 Samuel 21:15-17

- What strengths or weaknesses does David exhibit in each text?
- What is God's role in each text?
- Where would exiles see themselves in each of these texts?
- How would these stories foster hope in the hearts of exiles?
- How might these stories change the view of Israelites with regard to their captors?

Something Beautiful, Something Good

Bill and Gloria Gaither wrote a song titled "Something Beautiful." The chorus is composed of these words: "Something beautiful. Something good. All my confusion, He understood. All I had to offer Him was brokenness and strife. But He made something beautiful of my life."

The story of David and Bathsheba is a story of brokenness, confusion, and strife. And yet, God took a weak moment and redeemed it for divine purpose. While this should never prompt us to justify our unrighteousness, it should prompt us to recognize God's amazing grace. God is able to make something beautiful out of the worst and weakest moments of our lives.

- What sins might have been the source of Israel's banishment to Babylonian exile?
- What good could come from their time in exile?
- How might their lives and priorities be different when they are released from exile?

THE INTERPRETATION

Several years ago, the Muppets of *Sesame Street* performed a sketch titled "The King's Problem." All of the Muppets within the king's court were upset because the king's crown had fallen under his bed. How were they going to retrieve this valuable possession? They called the strongest man in the kingdom, but his strength couldn't help. They called the fastest man in the kingdom, but his speed was of no assistance. They called the wisest man in the kingdom, but he could not solve the problem. At the last tension-filled moment, a young servant girl walked into the room. She listened as the kingdom's most powerful men discussed the problem. Being the smallest in the room, she knelt down, crawled under the bed, and retrieved the crown. Everyone was amazed that someone so small and young and weak had the ability to solve such a great problem.

Weakness is relative—it is a relational tension. For one to know weakness, there must be an entity that, at least, appears relatively stronger. Some of our weaknesses are inherent; they are simply part of our individual genetic codes. Some of our weaknesses are the results of choice and circumstance. We all face the giants of loneliness, fatigue, loss, insecurity, and grief. We all pray and struggle to survive.

In our weakness, we, like the exiled Israelites, need to hear the stories of David. They remind us that "the selection process," God's prerogative to choose, offsets many of our weaknesses. As children of God, we are loved and cared for. We are precious and protected. And even in the exile of punishment, we are not alone.

If we have been fortunate enough to remain relatively strong in comparison to the world around us, then this means the world around us is relatively weak. As people of God, David reminds us to heighten our sensitivities to those who hurt. Look for the gifts and skills inherent in the relatively small and young and weak. Recognize that God does not always use the strongest or fastest or wisest. And when it is our time to pick the team, refuse simply to look at a person's outward appearance; choose to look at the heart. Be joyful in the fact that God has used you. Be joyful in the fact that you have gracefully survived. And offer the hope of survival to others.

Personal Reflections
- What have been some of the "high moments" and "low moments" of your life?
- How did these moments reveal your strengths and weaknesses?
- How did God help you survive the low moments?
- Who did you help during the high moments?

- Who do you consider "weak"? How can we, in our relative strength, be more sensitive and serving with regard to the needs of those who are weak?
- Look through your church hymnal and find songs that have helped encourage you during difficult times. How is our church hymnal similar to the Deuteronomic Historian's collected stories of David?

NOTES

[1] Walter Brueggemann, *First and Second Samuel*, Interpretation, A Bible Commentary for Teaching and Preaching (Louisville: John Knox Press, 1990), 120.

[2] Tony W. Cartledge, *I & II Samuel*, Smyth and Helwys Bible Commentary (Macon: Smyth and Helwys Publishing, Inc., 2001), 201.

[3] Ralph W. Klein, *I Samuel*, Word Biblical Commentary (Waco: Word, Incorporated, 1983), 162.

[4] Eugene H. Peterson, *First and Second Samuel* (Louisville: Westminster/John Knox Press, 1999), 94.

[5] Brueggemann, *Samuel*, 124.

[6] Bruce C. Birch, Walter Brueggemann, Terrence E. Fretheim, David L. Petersen, *A Theological Introduction to the Old Testament* (Nashville: Abingdon Press, 1999), 236.

[7] R. P. Gordon, *I & II Samuel* (Sheffield England: Sheffield Academic Press, 1994), 63.

Chapter Four

SURVIVING SPIRITUAL TENSION

GOD: COMMITTED BUT NOT CONTROLLED

Focal Text: 2 Samuel 24   Broader Text: 1 and 2 Samuel

Our high school literature class was scheduled to spend part of our semester studying a unit on drama. The majority of my eleventh-grade class (well, at least the guys) knew very little or cared very little for plays and playwrights. We had already spent a week butchering the Bard's romantic tale of Romeo and Juliet, when our patient pedagogue informed us we were moving on to a more modern work of literary art. She distributed copies of Thornton Wilder's *Our Town* to the less-than-eager class.

"Now," she asked, "who would like to play the part of the Stage Manager?"

The room was silent—uncomfortably silent.

"Michael, would you like to play the part?" she inquired.

"Well," he replied, "if I have to be in the play, I would rather have a starring role. I don't really think I want to be just a stage manager."

We all agreed that Michael, being the only guy who was interested in drama, should have a much more prominent role. Why would she want him to be a simple stage manager? Of course, in our unanimous agreement, we showed our complete ignorance of the Stage Manager's position within Wilder's classic work.

In the play *Our Town*, the Stage Manager is the lead character. While he is not directly involved in the actions of the other characters, he is quite present on the stage as an integral part of the drama. He verbally interacts with both actors and audience, helping move the play from scene to scene, season to season, and place to place. He not only sets the stage for each act and scene, but he also dictates and interprets their significance. The prominent role of the Stage

Manager—his existence within the drama—was a part of the genius of Wilder's classic work.

Our study of 1 and 2 Samuel has been built around the tensions experienced by the primary characters of these books: Samuel, Saul, and David. We could have chosen to orient our study around a series of other characters within the text. We might have chosen relatively obscure characters like Abner, Joab, and Nabal. Or we could have engaged in a study based upon the influence and faith of women within the text: Hannah, Abigail, and Bathsheba. Regardless of the series of characters chosen to provide a structure for our study, one character must be included in any list and receive our attention—God.

The lives of the kings and prophets within 1 and 2 Samuel merely orbit the greater mass of God's promises, judgments, words, will, and sovereignty.[1] Too often we read Scripture with little regard for this intricate role of God in the text. We assume God is somewhere behind every scene, somehow directing every character's movements. These assumptions, however, distract us from the rich detail of God's activity . . . and inactivity. They cause us to overlook, or at least undervalue, the biblical characters' doubts concerning the presence and role of God. It is, in fact, the presence and perceived absence of God in these books that lead to our final tension—the spiritual tension.

We are careful to call this a "perceived" sense of presence and absence because we are not trying to make an ontological statement concerning the reality of God's presence. The spiritual tension is more concerned with how people "feel," not with logical, theological, and systemic explanations. The spiritual tension is completely subjective, as opposed to the theological tension, which is based upon doctrinal objectivity. In other words, theology may teach us that God is omnipresent, but the biblical characters (and many of us modern-day characters) do not always feel the presence of God.

God has chosen the role of the Stage Manager. God has allowed his divine nature to be written into the drama of human existence. But God will not allow humanity to direct his action within the drama. God is willing to be committed to our drama, but not controlled within our drama. The Stage Manager must become a part of the play—intricately involved, yet possessing a self-directed will and presence. God moves us with limited verbal interaction from scene to scene, season to season, and place to place. And even when the divine seems absent, we trust that God still moves us toward some meaningful end. This was a truth the exiled Israelite needed desperately to embrace.

THE OCCURRENCE

Second Samuel 24 falls into the division of 2 Samuel that some scholars have called "The Samuel Appendix."[2] It is given this label because 2 Samuel 21–24 appear to be a miscellaneous collection of stories from different periods in David's reign that have been compiled and attached to end of the book. When I think of an appendix, however, my mind immediately moves toward the physiological image of an unnecessary appendage, which when infected often causes intense pain on the right side of the human body. (Or is it the left side?) But since this appendage has no particular function, it can be easily removed from the human body and never missed.

This physiological image is only partially true with regard to 2 Samuel 24. It is a painful text, but it is far from unnecessary. This is not a story randomly attached to end of the book because the Deuteronomic Historian, or some other contributor, couldn't find a better place for it. This is the final chapter. Samuel's story has been told. Saul's story has been told. David's story has been told. But God's story is not complete. God must intrude upon the story one more time. Divine presence must be reasserted in the story and in the world.

2 Samuel 24:1. Second Samuel 24 is a candid portrait of the God that has consistently moved in and out of the Deuteronomic Historian's narrative. It may not be the type of portrait you would paint of God, nor the type of portrait Israel would paint of God. But the Historian provides this last story to reinforce the image of God that he has observed in the life of Israel. The Deuteronomic Historian's portrait highlights the mysterious and uncontrollable nature of a committed God.

Chapter 24 begins by reminding us that the God of Israel has feelings. God is angry in v. 1. We are not sure why (which only adds to the mystery), but we know the anger is real. This anthropomorphic aspect of God's nature is not new to the Israelites. Those who embraced the Hebrew faith commonly spoke of God in anthropomorphic terms; they experienced a God that exhibited human characteristics and emotions. God is often described in Scripture with human physical features: the face of God, the hand of God, the mind of God, and the ears of God. In the past, the God of Israel had also employed human sensitivities: he heard Israel's cries, saw their suffering, and felt their pain (Exod 3:7-8).

If at times these divine attributes led to compassion, it made perfect sense that they could also lead to anger. God is a God that feels.

Complicating God's mysterious feelings is their unpredictability. Again, we do not know the cause of God's anger in v. 1. We just know God is angry. Sometimes God's anger seems to come in a moment. In 2 Samuel 6, David was having the ark of the covenant returned to Jerusalem. In the process of its movement, an attendant named Uzzah touched the ark; God immediately struck him dead. No warning, no lecture, no prophetic word—God immediately struck him dead.

The nation of Israel, on the other hand, practiced idolatry and engaged in numerous forms of injustice for centuries. Prophets came to warn them of God's impending wrath. Righteous kings were appointed to try and turn the tide of wickedness. God's patience seemed immeasurable before exile finally came.

We wish we could predict when grace gives way to anger. We wish we knew everything that made God angry. We wish we knew why God was angry in 2 Samuel 24:1. But these things are not ours to know. If we knew these things, God would be more predictable . . . and within our control. The mysterious God of Israel, however, refuses to be controlled, even with regard to his feelings.

The second half of v. 1 affirms God's continued activity in the life of the world. God's activity begins with the phrase "and (God) incited David." God's activity is certain, and certainly uncomfortable. God urges David to take a census of the people of Israel. We will later learn that God considers this to be a sinful act. Once David follows the "urging," "inciting,"—dare we say—"tempting" of God, God punishes the people for David's act. The idea that God would "lead someone into temptation" is so uncomfortable that a later historian retells the story in 1 Chronicles 21 and credits Satan with David's prompting.

The fact remains, however, that decades before the Chronicler interpreted David's act as satanically inspired and centuries before James told Christians that "God tempts no one" (Jas 1:13), the readers of 2 Samuel encountered the portrait of a God who incited David to do wrong. And why does this need to be reinterpreted? Why can't we trust the prayer of Jesus and say, "Lead us not into temptation"? (Matt 6:13, KJV).

While this text may seem problematic to us, it was not outside the boundaries of Hebrew thought. It was God who hardened the heart of Pharaoh within the Exodus tradition—an act that would later lead to Pharaoh's punishment. And later, in 1 Kings 22, God sends a lying spirit to entice Ahab into a war that will purposefully lead to Ahab's death. Second Samuel ends with the strong assertion that the God of Israel operates within no boundaries. God is free, unpredictable, beyond understanding, and dangerous.[3]

God is committed, but God will not be controlled.

2 Samuel 24:2-9. In vv. 2-9, we gain a hint as to why the census was considered sinful, as well as some insight into another caveat of God's continued activity. God is not only active through the practice of enticement; God also wishes to remain active in the defense of Israel.

It is commonly acknowledged that the primary purposes of taking a census in the ancient world were for the collection of taxes and the drafting of an army.[4] It seems that God tested David's confidence in divine protection and defense. Taxation and the expansion of the military would undergird the human forces in David's rule. But what would this say about God's role in David's military and might? The prophet Samuel once predicted that a king would take the people's sons to fight and run before the king's chariots (1 Sam 8:10-17). Could it be that God was tempting and testing to see if David would fall into that predicted pattern? David had relied on God's defense during his battle with Goliath and many subsequent engagements. Is this enticement designed to determine if David's days of trust have ended? God is willing and wanting to remain active in the defense of Israel.

2 Samuel 24:10-13. The verses that follow David's fateful decision remind the reader that God still speaks. As we will note later in our study, the frequency of God's word diminishes during the course of the Deuteronomic History. God's voice is heard often in the days of Moses and Joshua. God continues to speak to and through the judges who follow. Early in 1 Samuel, God converses regularly with Samuel and with David. But as the story progresses, we hear the voice of God less and less. Prophets are few and far between. Nathan confronted David's sin in 2 Samuel 12, but since then, the prophetic voice has been silent . . . until Gad.

God is not pleased with David's institution of the census. He sends the prophet Gad to offer David three options of punishment. David may choose three years of famine, three months of enemy pursuit, or three days of pestilence at the hand of God. As Samuel had prophesied (1 Sam 12:13-15), the actions of the king will be suffered or enjoyed by the people at large. Each of the options places the people at great risk. The good news, however, is that God still speaks. Options are given. The imminent pain will not seem random and without purpose.

2 Samuel 24:14-16. Not only is the mysterious God of Israel still feeling and acting and speaking, but the concluding verses of the Books of Samuel also affirm that God is still merciful. Although this final story concerns God's punishment for enticed sin, it is also quite clear about the possibility and availability of God's grace.

David obviously trusts God's potential for mercy. Given the three choices of punishments, David opts for pestilence at the hand of God. Why? "[L]et us fall into the hands of the LORD, for his mercy is great; but let us not fall into human hands." David knew that during a three-year famine the people of Israel would be at the mercy of the generosity of their neighbors. During three months of enemy pursuit they would be at the mercy of their adversary's sword. Rather than trust the mercy of humanity, David chooses to fall into the unpredictable and dangerous hand of God. David trusts that while God cannot be controlled, God is committed to Israel. Neighbors and enemies are predictably stingy and hostile. But with God, there is hope for mercy.

David's hope is vindicated and God's mercy is ultimately realized in v. 16. The angel of the Lord has followed a path from Dan to Beersheba to Jerusalem killing seventy thousand Israelites. As the angel approaches Jerusalem and prepares to spill its deadly pestilence there, God mercifully intervenes. The unpredictable God *repents*. No more information is given for God's mercy than was previously given for God's anger.[5]

2 Samuel 24:17-25. David responds to God's merciful act with a prayer of confession and repentance. At the insistence of the prophet Gad, David purchases the threshing floor of Araunah (the point at which the angel of the Lord had mercifully stopped) to build an altar and offer burnt offerings and peace offerings to the Lord. The chapter concludes with a reassurance of God's intention to avert the deserved pestilence from Israel. It must be noted, however, that God's mercy was not a result of David's sacrifice at the threshing floor of Araunah. Mercy had already been dispensed; bargaining and manipulation were not precipitating issues. These final words simply imply that David's prayers and eventual obedience were essential elements for God's continued mercy.

And so, the Books of Samuel conclude with God asserting himself as the main character of this historic narrative. What at first glance appears to be an appendix to the Deuteronomic History is actually a necessary reminder of God's continued empathy, action, conversation, and mercy with regard to Israel. Even when God seems absent from Israel's story, the divine Stage Manager is still there. God will not be controlled, but Israel is assured of God's commitment. Second Samuel 24 had the potential to speak volumes to the exiles in Babylon.

The Human Response

This chapter has intentionally focused our attention on the role of God within the text. David, however, represents the human role in relation to this mysterious and unpredictable God. Read the following texts again, giving attention to the verb associated with each. Consider how David responded to God. Are these verbs a part of our relationship with God? How do we use these verbs to relate to God? Can they be used in both positive and negative ways?

Choose—2 Samuel 24:1-9, 11-16
Confess—2 Samuel 24:10, 17
Worship—2 Samuel 18–25

THE MEMORY

Second Samuel 24 provided the exiled Israelites a much needed hope and assurance of God's continued presence and mercy. The spiritual tension created by God's apparently waning presence and haunting absence during their captivity in Babylon was no doubt overwhelming. Second Samuel's final chapter was needed to reverse the trend of God's diminishing role in their midst.

The diminishing role of God in Israel is a constant and important thread throughout the fabric of the Deuteronomic History. This fading of God's

> **The Ark of the Covenant**
> The ark was a portable sanctuary from Israel's wilderness days (see Exod 25:10-15). The ark was the place of God's special presence among the people, guiding them through the wilderness. It also served to house the two tablets of the Law (Deut 10:8) and hence had a specific link to the Sinai covenant. David recaptured the ark from the Philistines, brought it to Jerusalem, and built a house for it (2 Sam 4–6). This was a means that David used to unify the northern and southern tribes. King Solomon brought it into the Holy of Holies of the temple, where it symbolized not only the place of God, but the throne of God in the midst of his people (1 Kgs 8:1-13). The ark was probably destroyed by the Babylonians when they razed the temple, but no specific mention is made of its destruction.
>
>

presence is easily recognized by carefully observing God's symbol, God's word, and God's action in the text.

The primary symbol of God's presence in 1 and 2 Samuel is the ark of the covenant. This sacred box was constructed at Mt. Sinai following the Israelites' exodus from Egypt. Housed within its walls were the stone tablets containing the Ten Commandments and other holy relics. There is little doubt the Israelites equated the ark with the very presence of God. The "Song of the Ark" in Numbers 10:35-36 suggests that Moses addressed the ark as an embodiment of the Lord.

For all practical purposes, the ark was the presence of God in the minds of the people. It was carried before the people when they crossed the Jordan River into the land of Canaan. It was instrumental in the war against Jericho. It was present at the siege of other cities during the conquest of the promised land. In 1 Samuel 4, the Israelites lose a war against the Philistines and surmise that their loss is the result of the absence of the ark. Ironically, they retrieved the ark, entered another battle with the Philistines, and lost again! When the prophet Eli heard that the Philistines had captured the ark, he fell out of his chair, broke his neck, and died (1 Sam 4:18)! It was unthinkable that a foreign force could capture the very presence of God. (This could be an early hint, however, that the presence and power of God cannot be controlled . . . even by Israel.)

As powerful as the ark seemed to be, it began to lose its mystique through the course of time. David returned the ark to Jerusalem during the eighth year of his reign with much pomp and celebration. When in Jerusalem, it was placed in a tent for safekeeping. It did accompany David into one battle against the Ammonites (2 Sam 11), but David soon ordered its return to Jerusalem. There is no more record of its presence in the battles of Israel.

During the reign of Solomon (1 Kgs 8), Solomon placed the ark in the inner chamber of the newly built temple—the holy of holies. There is no further mention of the ark in the Deuteronomic History. This furnishing, which once embodied the power and presence of God, became an enshrined religious relic and at some point was eventually lost. It is easy to see the diminishing role of God in light of his most dominant symbol.

We can also observe the gradual decrease in God's presence through the reduced frequency of God's speech. The short phrase, "And the LORD said," comprises four percent of the Hebrew vocabulary.[6] Within the Hebrew Scriptures, we see this phrase fifty-three times in the Book of Exodus, twenty-eight times in the Book of Numbers, fifteen times in the Book of Deuteronomy (Are we noticing a pattern?), fifteen times in Joshua, fourteen times in Judges, thirteen times in 1 Samuel, and only four times in 2 Samuel. While the frequency of the phrase is not a scientific method of defining the limits of God's actual verbal exchanges in Israel's history, it at least suggests the writer's awareness that divine communication was in decline.

Finally, in addition to symbol and word, God's visibly recorded activity declined in the life of Israel. Prior to 1 Samuel 12, God is immanently intrusive in the drama of his world. God frequently inhabits the text as he creates, floods, delivers, provides, empowers, and blesses. But after the reign of Saul begins in 1 Samuel 13, there is much less divine activity. In the words of Old Testament scholar David Jobling, "Saul seems to inhabit a less God-filled world."[7]

This spiraling diminishment of God's presence comes to an abrupt halt in 2 Samuel 24. Absence is not the last word or the last feeling. God bursts back into the life of David and Israel and the exilic audience. God unpredictably and mysteriously reappears full of feeling, action, conversation, and grace. Second Samuel ends by affirming the existence and presence of a God who is willing to be committed but not willing to be controlled.

Through the Eyes of Exiles

C. S. Lewis was a great author and a lover of great books. In his letters to Arthur Greeves he once wrote, "I can't imagine a man really enjoying a book and reading it only once."[8] It is not uncommon for me to finish a book and then spend days rereading and reflecting upon significant lines and paragraphs.

Imagine that you are an exiled Israelite in Babylon. You have just finished reading 1 and 2 Samuel. As you reflect upon this collection of stories, think about the following questions.

- With which character did you most identify? Why?
- With which character did you least identify? Why?
- Which tension seemed most relevant to your life? Why?
- What stories helped you understand the nature of God?
- In what ways did people try to control God?
- In what ways did God exercise freedom?
- How do these insights into the nature of God offer hope to an exile?

THE INTERPRETATION

Maybe after years of exile and after hearing these stories over and over again, Israel finally learned the premiere lesson of human existence—we are servants of God, not vice versa. We exist for God's whims and not God for ours. We are at God's beck and call; God is not at ours. God is God. The God of Israel is committed to us but refuses to be controlled by us.

Each of the tensions we've encountered in 1 and 2 Samuel is a part of the mystery of God. God's embrace and rejection of political systems, the fine line God carves between law and grace, the push God gives the underdog, and the fluctuating sense of God's presence and absence all speak to the mysterious tensions inherent in a human relationship with the divine. These tensions keep God beyond our understanding. They keep us from reducing God to a manageable and predictable deity. They prevent us from carving an idol in our mind that resembles the God we wish God to be. The political, theological, relational, and spiritual tensions of these texts insure that God was and is and will always be a sovereign mystery.

Reunions

After ten years in the real world, my high school graduating class celebrated its reunion. Many of us had sporadically kept in touch, but few of us had spent the kind of time together we had during our academic days. It was a joy to see one another. We had obviously changed externally. But we had changed internally, as well. It was interesting to converse about values, feelings, and the variety of life experiences that had shaped us through the decade. There were also things we had forgotten about one another and the ten-year "refresher course" was an informative delight.

- What new aspect of God have you encountered during your study of 1 and 2 Samuel?
- Did you find this part of the nature of God refreshing or uncomfortable?
- How have you ignored this aspect of God in your personal theology and lifestyle?
- How do you plan to incorporate this aspect of God into your future beliefs and lifestyle?

Symbols

The ark of the covenant was a powerful symbol in the life of the ancient Hebrew. The Christian faith has its symbols as well. How have the following symbols fostered God's presence or sense of absence in your life?

- the cup and the bread
- a wedding ring
- the pulpit
- a candle
- the cross
- baptismal waters
- the empty tomb
- the manger

Control

The Israelites attempted to control the power and presence of God through their use of the ark of the covenant, ritualistic sacrifices, and an overreliance upon the doctrinal grace offered in the Davidic covenant.

- How do people try to control or manipulate God today?
- Is it possible to attempt to use prayer or worship as an instrument of divine manipulation?
- How are the promises of Scripture used to control and manipulate God? Is God bound by the promises of Scripture?
- How do we take advantage of God's grace in our living and decision-making?

NOTES

[1] Eugene H. Peterson, *First and Second Samuel* (Louisville: Westminster/John Knox Press, 1999), 91.

[2] R. P. Gordon, *I & II Samuel* (Sheffield England: Sheffield Academic Press Ltd., 1998), 95.

[3] Walter Brueggemann, *First and Second Samuel*, Interpretation, A Bible Commentary for Teaching and Preaching (Louisville: John Knox Press, 1990), 351.

[4] P. Kyle McCarter Jr., *II Samuel*, The Anchor Bible (New York: Doubleday, 1984), 514.

[5] Brueggemann, 353.

[6] Bonnie Pedrotti Kittel, Vicki Hoffer, and Rebecca Abts Wright, *Biblical Hebrew, A Test and Workbook* (New Haven and London: Yale University Press, 1989), 8.

[7] David Jobling, *I Samuel*, Berit Olam, Studies in Hebrew Narrative and Poetry (Collegeville: The Liturgical Press, 1988), 257.

[8] Walter Hooper, ed., *The Letters of C. S. Lewis to Arthur Greeves (1914-1963)* (New York: Collier/Macmillan, 1986), 439.

GLOSSARY

Amalekites—Recurrent enemies of the Israelite people, identified in Genesis 36:12 as descendants of Esau. Their first conflict with Israel occurred during the Israelite journey to Mt. Sinai following the exodus. Other clashes throughout the exodus story, the conquest of Canaan, and the establishment of the Israelite monarchy made this fierce tribal group perpetual enemies of Israel.

Ammonites—A tribal group descended from Lot who lived in a small kingdom northeast of the Dead Sea. During the exodus and the conquest of Canaan, the Ammonites were protected by God from Israel's sword because of their connection with Lot. During the period of the judges, however, the Ammonites began to oppress Israel and a perpetual animosity was stirred. Conflicts and battles with this tribe continued through the post-exilic era of Israel's history.

anointing—The pouring of sacred oil on the body, usually the head, of a person to symbolize the coming of God's spirit upon that person. The sacred oil was often produced by mixing aromatic spices and olive oil.

ark of the covenant—An Israelite cultic object, constructed at Mt. Sinai following the exodus, which served as a symbol of God's divine presence. This decorated wooden chest, which reputably contained the stone tablets on which the Ten Commandments were carved, was often carried before Israel into war. Later, it resided in the holy of holies of the Jerusalem temple.

Glossary

Babylonian exile—A period from 598–538 BC when the Israelites were separated from their homeland by the conquering Babylonian army. While their captive existence in Babylon was not always reported to be harsh, they were not allowed to resettle their homeland until Cyrus and the Persian army took control of Babylon in 539 BC.

Bethlehem—In Hebrew, the city name means "house of bread." This town, located about five miles south of Jerusalem, was the birthplace of David as well as the site of his anointment as king.

burnt offering—An offering in which the entire animal was burned on the altar. These offerings were often associated with petitions and the process of purification.

covenant—While often understood as a promise, pledge, or contract, biblical covenants are described in a variety of ways. A covenant is typically a solemn and binding agreement with specific obligations stated. Sometimes there are reciprocal obligations on the part of all parties involved. At other times, there may be self-imposed obligations by one party and/or demanded obligations on a secondary party.

Cyrus—The leader of the Persian Empire who successfully conquered the Babylonians and allowed the return of the Israelites to their homeland.

Deuteronomic Historian—A theoretic editor/writer who recorded the history of Israel from exodus to exile during the period of the exile. Most scholars agree that the Deuteronomic History includes the books of Deuteronomy, Joshua, Judges, 1 Samuel, 2 Samuel, 1 Kings, and 2 Kings.

Israel—This term is rarely used with regard to geographic and territorial designations. Rather, it more often refers to people groups. In its most generic usage, it refers to the descendants of Abraham, God's chosen people. After the death of Solomon, the nation of Israel divided. The southern kingdom, often referred to as Judah, was ruled by Rehoboam. The northern kingdom, referred to as Israel, was ruled by Jeroboam.

Judah—One of the sons of Jacob and eventually one of the tribes of Israel. Following the death of Solomon, Judah refers to the southern kingdom of the divided Hebrew nation.

judges—God-appointed individuals who provided guidance in judicial matters and military leadership after the exodus and prior to the establishment of the Israelite monarchy.

monarchy—The state of being governed by a sovereign king or emperor.

Nebuchadnezzar/Nebuchadrezzar—The king of Babylon from 605–562 BC. Both Judah and Israel were captured and exiled under his reign. Biblically, he is presented as an instrument of God's wrath against Israel who displayed remarkable moral and just qualities.

ontological—Refers to a state of being or existence.

peace offering—An offering presented to establish or maintain good relations with God. The priest and worshipers ate a portion of the animal burned. This meal symbolized unity between God and the people.

Philistines—A population of people who inhabited large coastal cities (Ashdod, Gath, Ekron, Ashkelon, and Gaza) on the banks of the Mediterranean Sea west of the Dead Sea. Their skill in weaponry and the manipulation of metals made them fierce and feared adversaries in Israel's history.

prophet—One who speaks for God. The role of the prophet in Hebrew Scriptures had more to do with proclaiming than predicting.

sovereign—The state of holding supreme authority and strength.

theocracy—The state of being governed by God/a god or by an official claiming divine sanction.

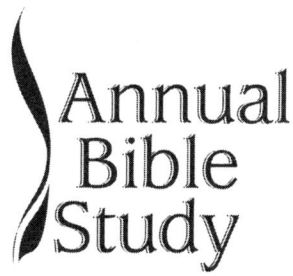

Wonder Is the Beginning of Wisdom.

Contact us and request a free sample kit. We have Sunday School resources for preschool, children, youth, and adults. Because it matters.
1-800-747-3016 • www.helwys.com/itmatters

Bible Study Matters.

Baptists are a people of the Bible, which means we take Bible study seriously. When we discover the wonder of the Bible, our ministries, our beliefs, and our lives are strengthened. That's why it's important to choose Sunday School materials that help children, youth, and adults grow in wonder and wisdom. Where you get your Bible study materials really does matter.

Baptist Values Matter.

Smyth & Helwys publishes materials based upon these Baptist principles:

- *The Lordship of Jesus Christ*
- *The authority of the Bible*
- *The priesthood of the believer*
- *The autonomy of the local church*
- *Respect for religious liberty*
- *The call of all Christians to ministry*
- *The importance of evangelism and missions*

Your Church Matters.

We work for you. Smyth & Helwys is a free press and not directed by any external group or denomination. We report not to trustees, but only to the local churches we serve. When you call on us, you will discover the strength of our commitment also to serve your church.

Discover More.
SMYTH & HELWYS

From Jerusalem to Gaza: An Old Testament Theology
B. Donald Keyser and H. Wayne Ballard

From Jerusalem to Gaza: An Old Testament Theology fills a void in the current literature on the theology of the Old Testament: It is accessible to students who are interested in the topic but who are not specialists. Therefore, it will be an ideal textbook for serious Bible students in Churches. Keyser and Ballard are a good team for this kind of book.

—*Danny Mynatt*
Associate Professor of Religion
Anderson College

Also available:

Faces of the Old Testament
Joseph A. Callaway

The Testimony of Poets and Sages
W. H. Bellinger Jr.

Journey to the Land of Promise
Page H. Kelley

Find these books and many others on the Old Testament at
www.helwys.com

You may also contact us by phone at 800-747-3016.